For Pictures At Night
Enlarged
Enlarging — Copying
Your Camera Examined, Cleaned Free
Name
Price
Here are
YOUR
SNAPSHOTS
Name
Spools
Prints
Enlgts
Price
FILM
WALLET
KEEP THIS BOOK IN A SAFE PLACE
Its loss may cause you trouble
BY GENESIS PUBLICATIONS

PHOTOGRAPH

Ringo

N'OUVRIR QU'EN CHAMBRE NOIRE !
NUR IN DER DUNKELKAMMER ÖFFNEN!
R
RINGO
Photograph Fotografera Genesis
Fotografia Foto Publications
Lichtbild Conmeditor Since
Photographie Valokuva 1974
ABRIR SOLAMENTE EN LA CAMARA OSCURA
OPEN ONLY IN THE DARKROOM !

This edition first published in 2015
by Genesis Publications

Printed and bound in China

10 9 8 7 6 5 4 3 2

ISBN: 978-1-905662-33-3

Genesis Publications Ltd
Genesis House, 2 Jenner Road
Guildford, England, GU1 3PL

Fine Books & Prints Since 1974
GENESIS-PUBLICATIONS.COM

The author has directly donated all royalties from the sale of this book to The Lotus Foundation. The publishers have also made a donation for each copy sold to the same charity.

LOTUSFOUNDATION.COM
The Lotus Foundation, 1st Floor, 90 Jermyn Street, London, SW1Y 4JD
Registered Charity No. 1070111 in England

Contents

I enjoyed taking pictures.

There's a lot of pictures in this book, shots of 'the boys' that only I could have taken. There are also photos of Dežo Hoffmann and Bob Freeman, photographers who took a lot of pictures of The Beatles. We always had a professional photographer to take photos of us, but I took pictures of them, too! I just loved taking pictures and I still do.

Photography has always been of interest to me. At one time, we all had cameras. That'd be an interesting thing, if everyone collected my photos, Paul's photos, John's photos and George's photos. We could have a book called 'The Beatle Photos': just an idea.

The good thing about this book is that it made me start looking through all my stuff. I found much more than I had anticipated. I never had an archive and I live in three countries, so it was all over the place. We looked on the internet for photographs and found a few there, and then we found a guy in San Diego who collected Rory Storm stuff, so he gave me a few. It was just incredible, the amount of material I've found, which is now safe.

We called Nick Roylance from Genesis Publications, because they did the *Postcards from the Boys* book. We sat down and put together a selection of photos and bits that are now in this book. That's how it came about – end of story.

Madryn Street, Liverpool, 1940

This is me as a baby.

I was very small as a baby. In fact, I wasn't that small – I was 10 pounds and I stayed the same weight!

There's no real shots of me till I was about 18, because we just didn't have cameras. There are a few baby photos, which you'll see in this book, but it wasn't like it is now.

I've got hundreds and hundreds of photos of my own kids. My daughter gets a bit miffed sometimes. Zak, being the first, has 20,000 photos of him. And Jason, being the second, has 10,000 of him. Then Lee, being the third child, has about five of her! 'There aren't a lot of photos of me, Dad!'

Admiral Grove, Liverpool, 1945

That's the street I moved to when I was five: Admiral Grove.

My house is the one with the 'v' for victory, from when the War was over. We even have, thanks to my mother, the rent book. The rent was 11 shillings a week – isn't that far out? – and then it went up to 11 shillings and three pence.

That was in 1954 – we'd been there nearly ten years by then. Before that we lived in Madryn Street, but my dad left when I was three, and we didn't have enough money to carry on living there. The house on Admiral Grove was classified derelict when we moved in, but we stayed there for years.

Admiral Grove was uglier than it looks in this photo. It was always dark because there was a big blank wall opposite, but it was great for the kids because they could kick a ball against it.

Eddie Miles lived next door and, later, we formed the Eddie Clayton Skiffle Group together. I lived in Admiral Grove until I was 23, to make life easy. Then I moved down to London with The Beatles, and George and I shared an apartment on Green Street in Mayfair. Very nice.

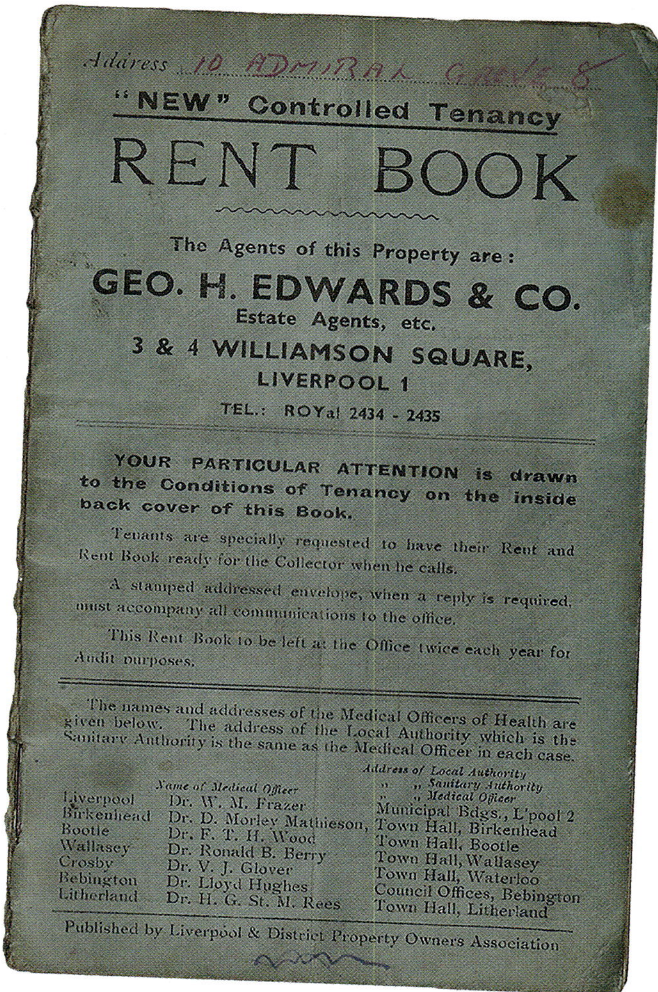

Address 10 ADMIRAL GROVE 8

"NEW" Controlled Tenancy

RENT BOOK

The Agents of this Property are:

GEO. H. EDWARDS & CO.

Estate Agents, etc.

3 & 4 WILLIAMSON SQUARE,

LIVERPOOL 1

TEL.: ROYal 2434 - 2435

YOUR PARTICULAR ATTENTION is drawn to the Conditions of Tenancy on the inside back cover of this Book.

Tenants are specially requested to have their Rent and Rent Book ready for the Collector when he calls.

A stamped addressed envelope, when a reply is required, must accompany all communications to the office.

This Rent Book to be left at the Office twice each year for Audit purposes.

The names and addresses of the Medical Officers of Health are given below. The address of the Local Authority which is the Sanitary Authority is the same as the Medical Officer in each case.

	Name of Medical Officer	*Address of Local Authority* / *" " Sanitary Authority* / *" " Medical Officer*
Liverpool	Dr. W. M. Frazer	Municipal Bdgs., L'pool 2
Birkenhead	Dr. D. Morley Mathieson,	Town Hall, Birkenhead
Bootle	Dr. F. T. H. Wood	Town Hall, Bootle
Wallasey	Dr. Ronald B. Berry	Town Hall, Wallasey
Crosby	Dr. V. J. Glover	Town Hall, Waterloo
Bebington	Dr. Lloyd Hughes	Council Offices, Bebington
Litherland	Dr. H. G. St. M. Rees	Town Hall, Litherland

Published by Liverpool & District Property Owners Association

St Silas's School, Liverpool, 1945-46

Well look at this. Here's a picture of me in school.

This is the class of 1945-46. I am in this photo, and it's up to you to find me.

I was taken to the school gate aged five by my mother. It was St Silas's School on High Park Street. It was a giant building, and there must have been 10,000 kids. There weren't that many, but that was my impression aged five.

I would walk home for lunch because we lived four minutes away. My mother said that one day I came home and told her that it was a half-day! She fell for it, until she saw all the other kids going back to school. So I had to go back.

I never liked school. For me, it was just something that you had to do. I had lots of breaks from it. When I was six I got very ill, so I was in hospital for over a year. I got back to school at about eight-and-a-half. Then, when I was 12, I had pleurisy, which later turned into tuberculosis, so I was off again. I didn't spend a lot of time in school, but we're not doing bad, are we?

Ritchie and Elsie Starkey, 1949

Me and my Mum.

I love that picture. The woman loved every second of my life, and remembered every second of my life. She was the best.

In Liverpool, if you had a party, everybody had to sing. That's how it was: it always ended up musical. Just to make my mum crazy, I would sing 'Nobody's Child'! And she'd sing 'The Little Drummer Boy'. My stepdad, Harry, was a great singer. He would sing Billy Daniels, Billy Eckstine – all the Billies. His big finale was always 'That Old Black Magic'. A lot of musical memories I have are from Harry.

Sentimental Journey wasn't just songs that my mum liked; it's what my stepdad and all my family sang at these parties. I made that record with George Martin after I left The Beatles, partly because I didn't know what else to do.

This is me in hospital the second time, with TB. That's Nurse Edge. She was so great to us all.

We used to rest in a glass ward in this parkland, to get all the fresh air. Where I came from, the air wasn't very fresh. There was lots of TB in our neighbourhood and, before streptomycin, whoever had it used to just sit in the living room and die. That was the answer; they just couldn't cure it.

I was in Liverpool Children's Hospital for my 14th birthday. I also had my seventh birthday in hospital, when I had peritonitis. I never had anything small. Appendicitis? No, peritonitis: where it explodes! So I had to spend another year in hospital.

I always thought, 'OK, I had my seventh birthday in hospital, I had my 14th birthday in hospital, maybe my 21st birthday?' But, hey, then a year later I joined The Beatles, so it was a lot better.

Tuberculosis time.

Look how close together the beds were! That's my mum visiting me in hospital in the background. She would visit whenever she could. When we were getting a bit better, they let us out of bed to play, and when they said, 'It's visiting time,' we'd all want to keep playing. That's just how kids are.

Because a lot of us stayed in bed a long time, they tried to keep us entertained. A woman came and she had a big board, with yellow and red marks on it. If she hit the yellow, you'd hit the tambourine; if she hit the red, you'd hit the drum. It was all percussion: tambourines, little drums and maracas. That was when I got a drum for the first time, and then I wouldn't be in the hospital class band unless I was given the drum after that! I was in the ward, hitting my drum, going, 'Oh no, I'm not playing tambourine!'

It was like a magical moment. From then on, I only wanted to play drums. It was really far out how strong that urge was. It was like a gift from God, really, 'You will be a drummer!' The hospital year went on forever, but something good came out of it.

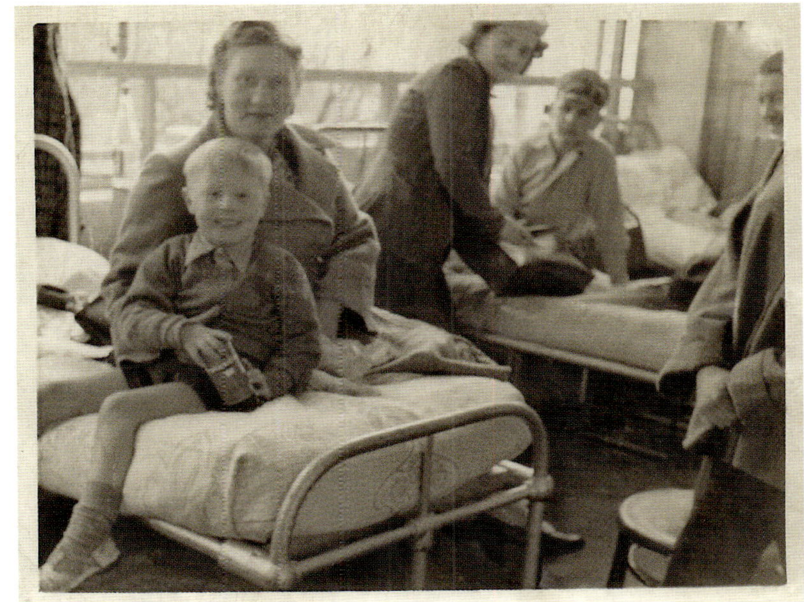

THE UNITED LIVERPOOL HOSPITALS
ROYAL LIVERPOOL CHILDREN'S HOSPITAL
TELEGRAPH ROAD HESWALL

ADMIT ONE VISITOR

Patients Name Richard Starkey

Ward Hugh Owen Thomas Ward

Date of Issue 16-8-'54

THIS CARD MUST BE PRODUCED EACH VISITING DAY

There's me, patting the Horse Guard's horse.

We sort of conned my way out of hospital so I didn't have to be there for my 15th birthday. We went down to Romford, where my stepdad's family lived. His dad was great, and he knew London like the back of his hand. We went walking all over London and saw the sights, the British Museum and the Searchlight Tattoo. It was a great day out, but it was a bit long for someone who'd just come out of hospital.

Here I am with my stepfather's dad, on Tower Bridge.

This is the ticket from getting the train to White City, when I went to see the Searchlight Tattoo.

It had all the Army bands playing, tanks coming on and guys fixing guns. One of the best musical moments of my whole life happened that day. There was a sound offstage: it was the American Air Force band, and they came on swinging. I remember being so excited; I loved that band. It was a beautiful moment for me that I'll never forget. I had another one before that, when I heard Gene Autry singing 'South of the Border'. It blew me away!

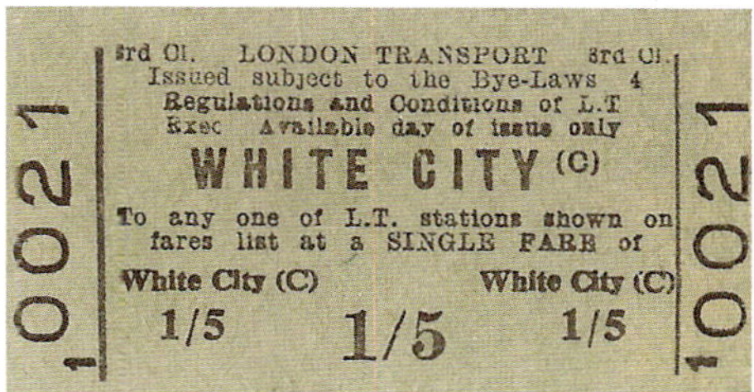

This is all stuff that my mother kept.

We found lots of photos and then we found my mother's box. She was such a hoarder – who knew? When she died, I just took the boxes and put them in our attic; I didn't really look at them. When we opened them up, we found these two ticket stubs, as well as some incredible stuff from when I was in Germany. I must have brought these things back, in my pocket or in my case, and she'd put everything in a little tin.

This is Davy Patterson and me.

We went to New Brighton when I came out of hospital. We put our heads in the holes, and here we are as 'native boys'. I don't know if you can do this now; remember this was the Fifties.

I found an Ajax drum kit at Frank Hessy's music shop in Liverpool. That's the hire purchase agreement that didn't go through because I borrowed the money instead. The kit was going to cost £57, the whole deal, but with the hire purchase it was going to be £68. So I thought, 'I'll borrow off my granddad anc save 11 quid.' I paid him back a pound a week, from working in a factory. It made me feel good that I did actually pay him back.

My granddad was a great guy. The first time I came out of hospital, he bought me a harmonica, but I had no interest in it. We also had a piano, but again, no interest. I only wanted to play drums.

The first kit I got wasn't Black Pearl, like I'm known for, but it was similar. Then I got a Premier kit, and then a Ludwig. I loved Ludwig, mainly because they were American. The drums are great, but when I looked at them in a shop window in London, and it said, 'Ludwig American drums'... Wow!

That's the first time I had a real kit and then it went on from there. Now I get them for free. It's weird: when you can afford your own kit, they want to give them to you. But I stuck with Ludwig because I still like the sound.

The first job I had was working on the railways.

I delivered notices to factories that their goods were at the station, and I lasted five weeks. I really went there to get a suit and some warm clothes, because it was freezing, but they only gave me a hat so I was pretty disappointed.

That didn't last, so I went to work on the St Tudno pleasure boat. It went from Liverpool to Llandudno every day; it left at ten and was back at eight every night. I actually went on that boat because I wanted to be in the Merchant Navy. There were a lot of guys in our neighbourhood in the Merchant Navy, going to see new places, and I thought, 'How great is that?'

One day when I was working, they wanted me to load the bar with the crates of beer. I wouldn't, because I had my best suit on, and so they fired me. But before that, I'd go into the pub and try to pick up girls. When you're 18, you're always trying to pick up chicks, that's just how life is.

They'd say, 'What do you do?'

I'd say, 'Oh yeah, I just got back.'

'Where were you?'

'Llandudno.'

They'd say, 'Oh, when did you leave?'

I'd say, 'Ten o'clock this morning!'

'Piss off!'

It worked sometimes, though.

They were my first two jobs: the railway and the boats. If ever I was out of work, it was OK because my mother went to the pub and asked around, and I would have a job the next day. I just had to go and see somebody, and then I was working again. In those days, you had to work. That was just how it was: you had to get up and get to work.

So when this job ended on the boats, my mother went to the pub and got me a job at H. Hunt & Son. It was great because it was just down the road, so I could get up at a quarter to eight in the morning and be in work by eight. But then the buggers moved to Speke, which was a ten-minute walk to the bus and a half-hour bus ride. That was a bit of a downer, but I stayed there, and that's where I started playing drums.

When I was at H. Hunt & Son being an apprentice engineer, I had to go to a technical college to learn how to draw blueprints and take measurements. I got 84 percent for my attendance, and they still wanted me to repeat the course! Out of the 259 hours I could have done, I completed 218 and a half – so give me a break, brothers! The subject I really lost in was English, but I was great at Engineering Drawing, so if you ever want me to draw you something...

CITY OF LIVERPOOL EDUCATION COMMITTEE

RIVERSDALE TECHNICAL COLLEGE

DEPARTMENT OF ENGINEERING

PROGRESS and ATTENDANCE REPORT

OF

RICHARD STARKEY

DURING THE SESSION 1958 – 1959

in the PREPARATORY ENGINEERING P.S.1A

PART TIME DAY ~~AND/OR EVENING~~ COURSE

Registered Attendance	SUBJECT	Home-work %	Class-work %	Examination Marks %	REMARKS
DAY	WORKSHOP PRACTICE				
Possible Hours 259	TECHNOLOGY				
Actual Hours 218½	ENGINEERING DRAWING	53	63	40	
Percentage 84	MATHEMATICS	50	64	—2—	
EVENING	ENGINEERING SCIENCE	16	21	10	
Possible Hours	ENGLISH	15	35	30	
Actual Hours					
Percentage					

No student will be permitted to transfer to the next year of the course in the following session unless the Principal and the Examining Body concerned are satisfied that he has attended regularly and punctually, and has reached a satisfactory standard, not only in the Sessional Examinations, but also in Homework, Classwork, Laboratory and/or Workshop.

Recommendation REPEAT COURSE

Enrolment 7th to 11th Sept 1959 – 9 a.m. to 4 p.m.

A L Martin
Head of Department

A. R. KINSMAN, B.Sc., (Eng.), A.M.I.E.E., A.M.I.Mech.E.
Principal.

M. 1917

Dick, Mick and Rick.

That's the office party at H. Hunt & Son, where we'd all get dressed up and usually get drunk and swear at the bosses. Then we'd go into work after the Christmas holiday and start making friends again.

Mick is in the middle, I don't know the guy on the left, and I'm on the right.

Dancing with a girl I knew called Geri.

My next-door neighbour's real name was Eddie Miles, but he called himself Eddie Clayton. He was just one of those guys who could play anything, so he started playing guitar. I had a snare drum, so I became the snare drummer, and then our friend Roy Trafford made a tea-chest bass. They were the first instruments we had, and that was my first band: the Eddie Clayton Skiffle Group.

We started playing for the guys at work in the basement at lunch hour, and then we got a few gigs and entered competitions, like 'The Best Skiffle Band in Liverpool'. Then we moved on a bit, playing pubs and clubs and weddings. We would play anywhere. We weren't very good players, but we tried our best. That's how it all started.

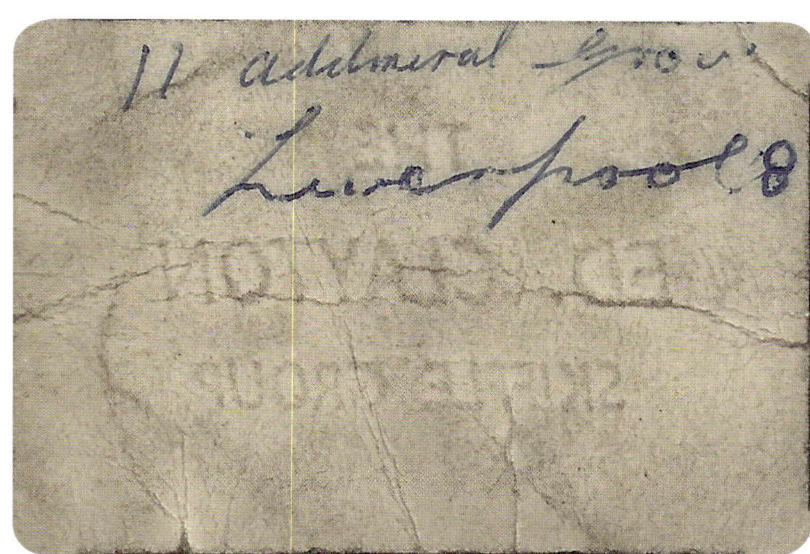

Rory Storm

and the

Hurricanes

PRESENTED BY:–
Phone:
STOneycroft 3324

Downbeat Promotions
54 Broadgreen Road
Liverpool 13

National Finalists	*Liverpool Empire ....*	*1957/58*
People £5,000 Finalists	*Butlins ....*	*1958/59*
Villa Marina (Winners)	*I. O. M. ....*	*1959*
Marion Ryan Show	*Rhyl ....*	*1959*
Carol Levis Final .... (Group Winners)	*Liverpool Empire ....*	*1959*

Rory Storm and the Hurricanes were the biggest band in Liverpool at the time.

They were the third band I was in. I started with the Eddie Clayton Skiffle Group, then I went to the Darktown Skiffle Group, and then I joined Rory.

With Rory, we were playing less skiffle and moving into rock. We got thrown off at the Cavern because we were traitors to skiffle! Johnny Guitar brought a big radio down and plugged his guitar into it. We got thrown off, but we didn't care. We were 18 or 19, so we could do what we liked. 'We're gonna play rock!' We may have been fined as well. Rory dealt with the money. He was our booker and lead singer, and he would get us to the gig.

Cavern Club, Liverpool, November 20th 1959

That's the first ever shot of me playing at the Cavern, and that's Johnny Guitar.

Johnny Guitar was like the first Jimi Hendrix in my life; I thought he was incredible.

These are not my drums. The snare and the sticks would have been mine, but I never had a white kit.

Out on the town with a couple of nice ladies.

This is a mixed bag of photobooth shots.

This is me with the Butlins sign, on our first trip to Butlins in Pwllheli.

In 1960, I was playing with Rory Storm and still working in the factory, when we got a three-month gig at the Butlins holiday camp in Wales. Everyone in my family was disappointed, because I was going to Riversdale Technical College and working as an apprentice, and I could have come out of that with a piece of paper that said I was an engineer. That would have been big news in our house, that anyone would have passed anything.

It was a big decision to leave college. It wasn't so huge to me, but it was a huge decision for my mum, my stepdad, and all my aunties and uncles. There was a little consternation at home – it was like a family gathering. They said, 'It's all right as a hobby, son,' but I said, 'No, this is what I'm going to do,' because I just loved to play. I made that decision and I've played ever since. It was a pivotal moment in my life.

I always remember that the foreman at H. Hunt & Son said, 'You'll be back, and you'll be brushing the floor because you'll have lost your gig as an engineer.' Anyway, I drove back in my Zodiac, showing off! We were getting paid daily, so I could say, 'I'm a musician now.'

In bed at Butlins.

Johnny Guitar and I shared a chalet, ten foot long by eight foot wide. Ah, the chalets of early Butlins...

Here we are at Butlins again.

When we went to Butlins, we all changed our names. I was being called 'Rings' in Liverpool, because I wore a lot of rings, so I became 'Ringo Starkey'. But that didn't really work, so I just took the '-key' off and called myself 'Ringo Starr'. This is Johnny Guitar, and we also had Ty O'Brien, Lu Walters and Rory Storm. So that's how it happened and my name has been Ringo ever since.

'Starr Time' was my great idea because I used to like to sing, too. I'd do 'Watch Your Step' and 'Alley Oop', and a couple of other rock 'n' roll numbers. It meant that Rory could have a break – he'd say, 'Ladies and gentlemen: Ringo's "Starr Time".'

ISER-KELLER
nzpalast der Jugend

Being lads in Hamburg was just the most exciting time.

And we got to know The Beatles a lot better. They played the Bambi Kino and we played the Kaiserkeller, then Koschmider put us both in the same club. We had the battle of the bands every night and would end up having a few drinks together or whatever, and we became friends.

The first meal I had in Germany was with Stuart Sutcliffe, who took me to Chug-ou's Chinese restaurant. They did huge pancakes – '*pfannkuchens*'. That was our one meal for the day because we weren't getting a lot of money.

I met Astrid Kirchherr and Klaus Voormann in Hamburg. They were the student university crowd. They loved it when I did 'Alley Oop', because in any language 'Alley Oop' means something. It was a comedy song and they'd all join in, 'There's a man in the funny papers we all know, Alley Oop Oop.' I got to know Astrid and Klaus because they would always request it. In the clubs, people would get drunk and request songs, sometimes in a very strong manner. They'd send crates of beer or champagne up if they were having a good time. And then some hard guy would come right to the front and say, 'You spielen what I say!'

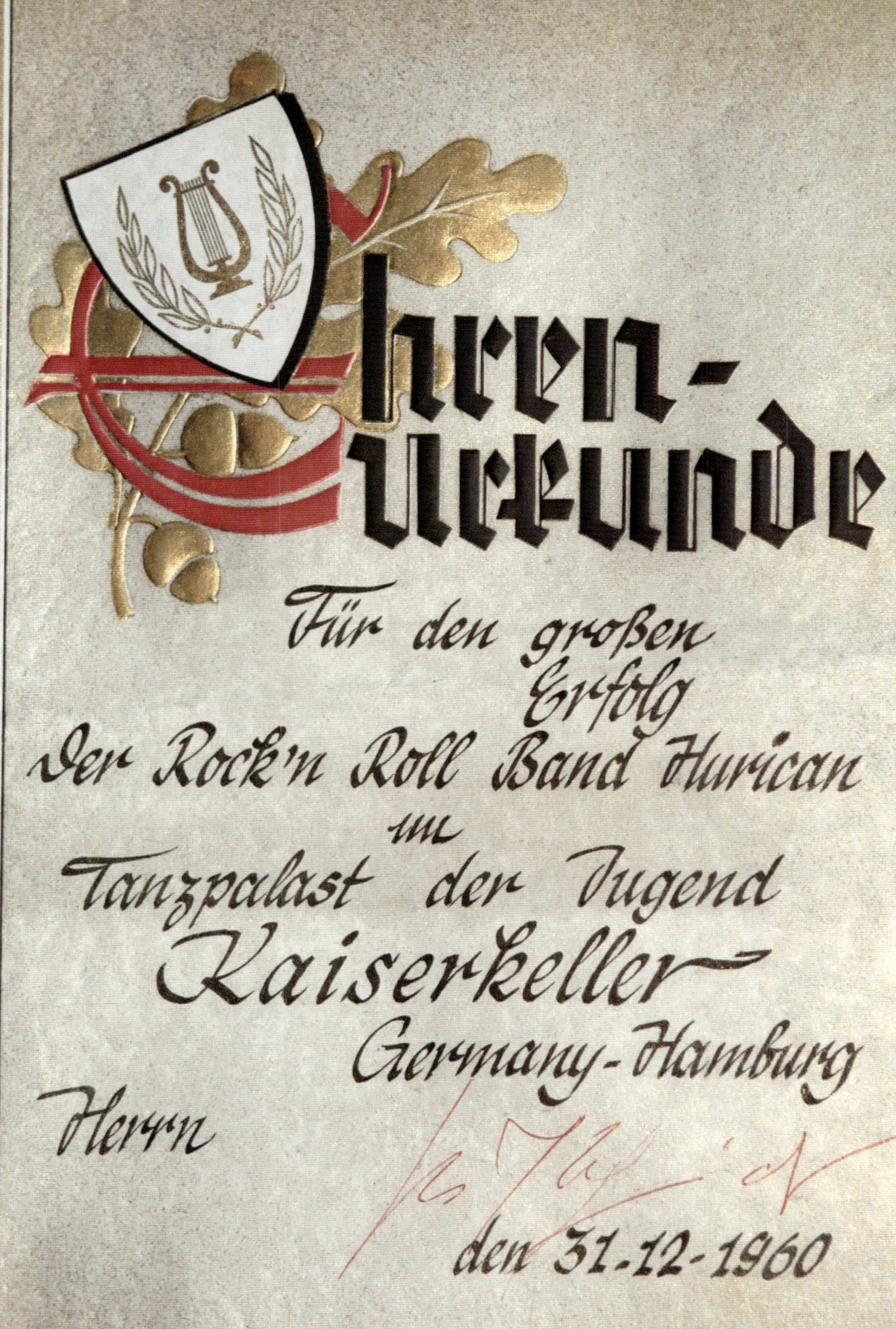
Ehren-
Urkunde
Für den großen
Erfolg
der Rock'n Roll Band Hurican
im
Tanzpalast der Jugend
Kaiserkeller
Germany-Hamburg
Herrn
den 31-12-1960

This is a crowd of different Liverpool bands, all together.

I'm in the middle, there's Johnny Hutch and Lu Walters; just a gang of lads hanging out. Howie Casey always wore that trilby and a long mac or overcoat.

I truly believe that the music came out of Liverpool because there was no call-up: if you were born after September 1939, you didn't go in the Army automatically. So, around 1957, when that law came in, we all picked up instruments and started playing them. Everybody was playing something and bands were in every household. That's why it all started.

Rory Storm and the Hurricanes, Liverpool Stadium, May 3rd 1960

An all-night session.

I'm afraid that, besides Johnny Guitar, I don't remember any of these people. It was an exciting time, because we'd hang out and talk music with everybody. There were the coffee bars and The Jacaranda Club. They used to book a trio for the all-night sessions, because at midnight every band in Liverpool would come down – and we would all play for free – so it was a cheap trick to just pay a trio. We just wanted to play, so we would play day and night, and be up all night. It was like 'music, music, music', and I loved it.

Admiral Grove, Liverpool, July 7th 1961

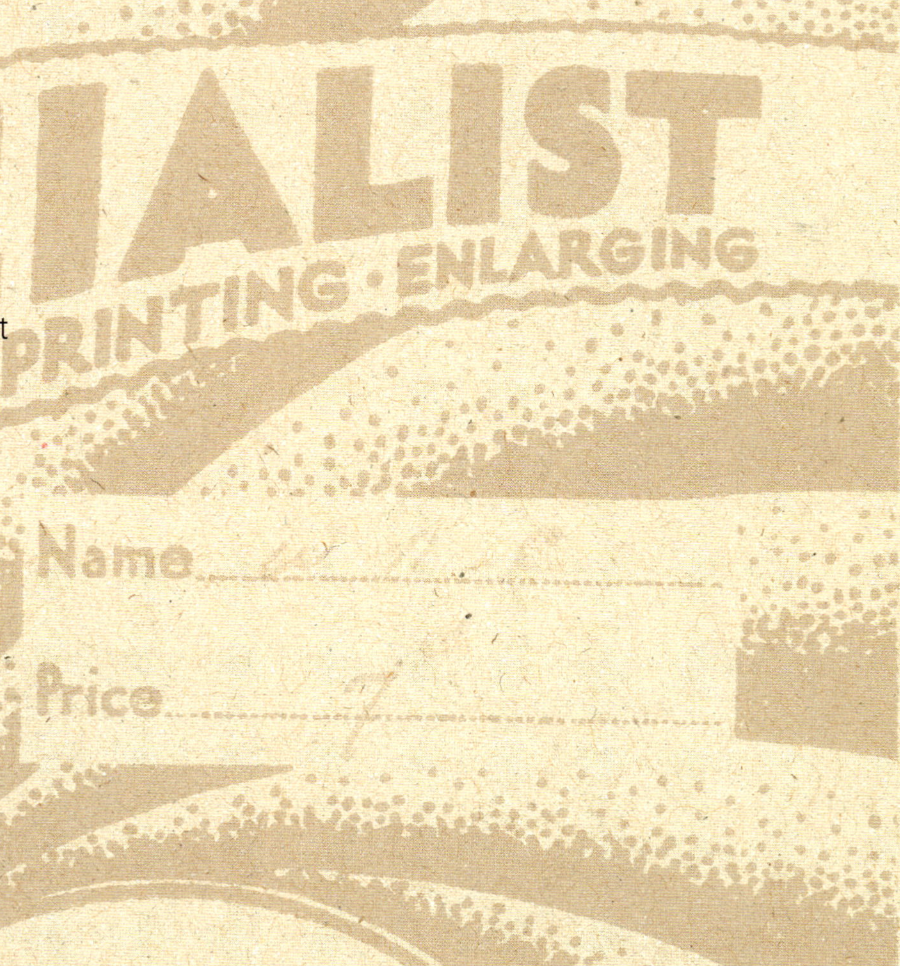

At my 21st birthday.

I lived in a very small house, and we crammed about 80 people in there. That's a picture of us all on this wasteland, right opposite our front door. There used to be a block of horrendous flats, and we had a big blank wall in Admiral Grove, but eventually they knocked them down.

We used to call it a bombsite, but the bombs didn't actually hit it. They hit a lot of places around where I lived during the War. We thought of them as playgrounds for the kids.

There's a woman in here, my mum's best friend, Annie McGuire. She was so great because I'd be tapping around in the house and she'd say, 'I'll see you on the Palladium, son!' She was always giving me a good push. You remember things like that, because there were a lot of people saying, 'Keep the noise down.'

There's Cilla Black and some of The Big Three: Johnny Hutch, Johnny Gustafson and Adrian Barber.

Cilla and half of Liverpool were performers. I'd given up working by then, but most people still had regular jobs, and Cilla worked in an office. We would always ask her to get up and sing. Then when Brian Epstein became our manager, he managed a lot of acts in Liverpool, including Cilla. That's how she got that job on TV and she still talks in her Liverpudlian accent.

Johnny Hutch was a cool drummer; it was only Johnny and I that could really play in Liverpool!

This picture blows me away.

It's just me with my mum and stepdad, Elsie and Harry, having a bit of fun outside the house. But I'm wearing Birkenstocks, how cool am I? Birkenstocks! In those days! When I saw that picture I was like, 'What? Where did I get them?'

Another night out, another party, another something.

Ey, another night out, thank you, Lord! Next.

Oh, another night out, thank you, Lord! Next.

MON 22/5/61

JAZZ

JIVING AT THE O.P.B.

TO-NIGHT!! TO-NIGHT!!

THE RORY STORM FAREWELL SHOW

Positive last appearance of this Group prior to summer engagements. with Three Guest Groups

CLIFF ROBERTS AND THE ROCKERS
ROCKING ROBIN AND THE RAVENS
CARL VINCENT AND THE COUNTS.

7.30 to 11.30 p.m., 3/-.

ORRELL PARK BALLROOM

TO-NIGHT! TO-NIGHT!

LITHERLAND TOWN HALL

Cliff Roberts. Ravens. Karl Terry's Cruisers Del Renas. 7.30-11.30 p.m.
Admission 3/-.

Saintes Amphitheatre, France

It's Rory Storm and the Hurricanes in a Roman arena.

We were on our way to play the American army bases in Fontenet, in France. We got the train to Paris, but some *gendarmes* with machine guns threw us off the train; they were having an upset with Algeria or somewhere in those days. We didn't have any money, so we had to hock my drums to get a room for the night. We got money sent to us, got the drums back and carried on our journey!

We went and played the American bases and it was great. We were in our twenties and this was all such a big adventure.

Rory and the boys. We've all got
Roman laurel wreaths on our heads!

We didn't have a girl in the band, but we had to take one with us for the soldiers.

This was a big gig for us. I remember seeing Jerry Lee Lewis at the New Brighton Tower Ballroom. It was a great venue, but it was cavernous. The echo would come back, so you'd have to watch what you were playing to, so that you didn't start playing to the echo. Anyway, nothing's better than playing. You can see there's a speaker there, but I can't see the amps. If you look at the Beatle pictures, the amps weren't big at all.

Little Richard played the Tower Ballroom on the same bill as us. My God, he was so great! He's still great today. I remember the first time I heard him. It was on Alan Freed's show on Radio Luxembourg. They had one half-hour show every Sunday, and they would play rock 'n' roll. At four o'clock on Sunday, my mate Roy and I listened to that show. It didn't matter what was going on, that's what we did. That was the first time I heard any real rock 'n' roll on the radio. The BBC wouldn't play it.

Promotional Posters, 1961

I put this photo in because of the posters.

There's one of Emile Ford, who sang 'What Do You Want to Make Those Eyes at Me For?' There's also the poster for the Big Beat at the Tower Ballroom, which had The Beatles, Rory Storm, and Gerry and the Pacemakers, among other bands.

Gerry and the Pacemakers sung 'You'll Never Walk Alone', which is the anthem of Liverpool. They ended up as one of Brian's acts and we were all good pals. Brian had Gerry, The Beatles, Cilla and all these people. When we did Christmas shows there would be five or six of us all on the same bill, so we just hung out, and then we'd go to clubs at night. Liverpool was great because there were so many bands, and after the gig we'd all meet up, or go to each other's gigs and play. That's what it was about. Just playing was the deal.

I played a gig where three bands were playing on the same bill. We would each play for an hour, in two half-hour sets. Just by chance, the drummers for the other two bands didn't turn up. I played with Rory, then the next band came on, and when the curtains opened, I was there again! The curtains closed, opened up again: I was with the next band! We knew the numbers and we all knew each other, so it was fun.

Top Ten Club, Hamburg, 1962

There I am with Tony Sheridan and Roy Young, and Colin the Policeman is on bass.

I don't know if he passed the course, but we always called him Colin the Policeman. Roy Young taught me how to play boogie-woogie on piano, and I still play it today.

The crazy thing when I played with Tony Sheridan was that if anybody talked to his girlfriend, Rosie, he'd put his guitar down, run off the stage, jump down into the audience and fight the guy! So we would just carry on playing! We'd be jamming away and he'd be punching and fighting, and then he'd come back on stage and just carry on like nothing happened.

PUTTING GREEN, BUTLIN'S HOLIDAY CAMP, SKEGNESS PN292

BUTLIN'S, SKEGNESS
A night scene

It was so exciting that we got to play six nights a week. We had Saturday off – that's when they changed the holidaymakers coming in and going out. I always used to go in the Rock 'n' Calypso Ballroom. We were so excited.

SKEGNESS

Dear Els and Harry

Having a great time on the tour we are next to top of the bill

My cold has cleard up fine now so dont be ~~[illegible]~~ worrying about me

I have got ten tickets for the show 8 together at 7/6 and two at 8/6 thay are being sent to you somtime well see you on the 24th

Love Richy

xxx

THE BEATLES

Details of engagements week commencing 19.8.62

Sunday	19th	August	CAVERN CLUB (T.V. Representative in attendance)
Monday	20th	"	MAJESTIC BALLROOM, CREWE Equipment to arrive by 7.15 and group no later than 7.45. Sincerely hope that a lasting impression will remain in Crewe following this last performance.
Wednesday	22nd	"	Midday CAVERN CLUB (There may be speciall arrangements in connection with this performance - details later)
"	"	"	Evening CAVERN CLUB
Thursday	23rd	"	RIVERPARK BALLROOM, CHESTER It may be necessary to try a little harder in Chester to win 'em over in this charming Cathedral City ! Equipment to arrive by 7.15 p.m. and group to be present in the ballroom no later than 8.15 p.m.
Friday	24th	"	Midday CAVERN CLUB
"	"	"	Evening MAJESTIC BALLROOM, BIRKENHEAI Equipment to arrive by 7.15 p.m. and group by 8.30 p.m.
Saturday	25th	"	MARINE HALL, BALLROOM, FLEETWOOD Equipment to arrive by 7.0 p.m. and group no later than 7.30 p.m.

Paul and me on holiday in Tenerife.

We'd go on holiday and it was great; we could go away, have a good time and be left alone. I do feel sorry for the kids these days. Although a lot of them court the press and pose for them, it's really very hard for anyone well known to get away completely. We could at least go on holiday, and that was a great one. Klaus Voormann's dad had a house in Tenerife, which is why we went there.

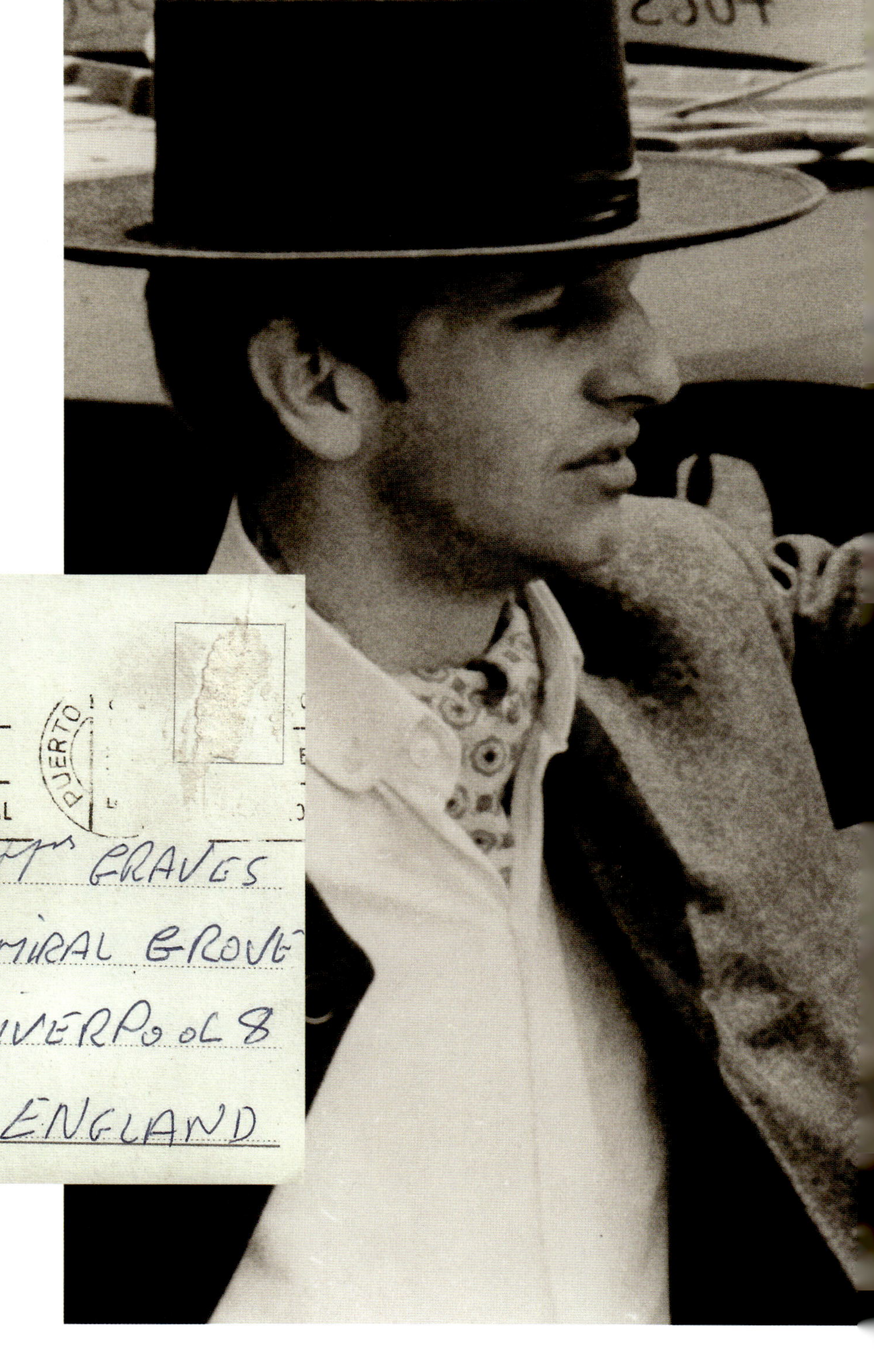

Dear Elsie and Harry
arrived hear OK. the plane was fab the house we are staying in is great the weather is good having a fab time see you soon
Love Richy xxx
P.S. WENT TO A BULLFIGHT YESTERDAY

GRAVES
10 ADMIRAL GROVE
LIVERPOOL 8
ENGLAND

LAS CARTAS PARA MADRID Y BARCELONA DEBEN LLEVAR EL NUMERO DE SU DISTRITO POSTAL

27 PUERTO DE LA CRUZ - TENERIFE.
Avenida de Cristóbal Colón y Piscina de San Telmo.
Columbus Avenue and San Telmo Swimming-pool.
Avenue Colomb et Piscine San Telmo.
Viale Colombo e Piscina San Telmo.

Foto: Martín Herzberg Depósito Legal B. 9765.-1959

DISTRIBUIDOR EXCLUSIVO: SUCESOR DE VÍCTOR GONZÁLEZ DELGADO. - PLAZA CANDELARIA, 4 - TEL. 3725 - SANTA CRUZ DE TENERIFE. PROHIBIDA SU REPRODUCCIÓN

BHAILE ÁTHA CLIATH
NOV 1963
CEADANNA

ÉIRE

AN tACHT UM THRACHT AR BHOITHRE, 1933.
ROAD TRAFFIC ACT, 1933.

CEADUNAS TIOMANA.
DRIVING LICENCE.

DUBLIN CORPORATION
4, KILDARE ST.,
DUBLIN, 2.

K 815615

CONTAE (no CONTAE-BHUIRG)
COUNTY (or COUNTY BOROUGH) ....

Ainm agus Sloinne an Cheadúnaí
Full name of Licensee .... Richard J. Starkey

Seoladh an Cheadúnaí
Address of Licensee .... 2 M. Hatch St.
.... Dublin, 2.

Aois an Cheadúnaí
Age of Licensee 5/7/1

An dáta ar ar rugadh an Cheadúnaí
Date of birth of Licensee ....

Tréimhse Dhleathachta
Period of Validity

On
From the .... 8th adh lá de
day of .... Nov 19 63

go dtí an
up to and including the .... 7th adh lá de
day of .... Nov 19 66
agus an lá san d'áireamh.

Ceadúnuítear leis seo mar leanas don té atá ainmnithe thuas, ar feadh na tréimhse dleathachta luaidhtear thuas ach an ceadúnas do bheith sighnithe aige :—

The person named above provided he has signed this licence is hereby licensed during the above-mentioned period of validity as follows :—

(a) má tá no nuair a bheidh sé bliana déag slán ag an duine sin ach é bheith fé bhun seacht mbliana déag d'aois, mótar-rothar do thiomáint, agus

(b) má tá no nuair a bheidh seacht mbliana déag slán ag an duine sin ach é bheith fé bhun ocht mbliana déag d'aois, aon tsaghas mótar-fheithicle éadtruime do thiomáint, agus

(c) má tá no nuair a bheidh ocht mbliana déag slán ag an duine sin ach é bheith fé bhun bliain agus fiche d'aois, aon tsaghas feithicle inneall-ghluaiste do thiomáint ach amháin mótar-fheithicil throm no inneall gluaiste le linn paisnéirí bheith á n-iompar ar an bhfeithicil no ar an inneall gluaiste sin ar luach saothair, agus

(d) má tá no nuair a bheidh bliain agus fiche slán ag an duine sin, aon tsaghas feithicle inneall-ghluaiste do thiomáint.

(e) má bhaineann alt 26 (2) den Acht san thuas leis an duine sin, aon chineál feithicle innealighluaiste do thiomáint go mbeidh sé, de bhuadh an fho-ailt sin, i dteideal é do thiomáint.

(a) if or when such person has attained the age of sixteen years and is under the age of seventeen years, to drive a motor cycle, and

(b) if or when such person has attained the age of seventeen years and is under the age of eighteen years, to drive any kind of light motor vehicle or motor cycle, and

(c) if or when such person has attained the age of eighteen years and is under the age of twenty-one years, to drive any kind of mechanically propelled vehicle except a heavy motor vehicle or a locomotive while such vehicle or locomotive is actually carrying passengers for reward, and

(d) if or when such person has attained the age of twenty-one years, to drive any kind of mechanically propelled vehicle.

(e) If such person comes within Section 26 (2) of the above Act, to drive any class of mechanically propelled vehicle which he is entitled to drive by virtue of that sub-section.

Sighniú an Oifigigh do thug amach
Signature of Issuing Officer. .... F. X. Hurley

FOGRA.

Beidh sé de dhualgas ar an gceadúnaí, chó luath agus do gheobha sé an ceadúnas so, é do shighniú sa spás atá ann chuige sin. Ní bheidh aon éifeacht ag an gceadúnas go dtí go sighneofar amhlaidh é.

NOTICE.

It is the duty of the licensee, immediately he receives this licence, to sign it in the space provided for the purpose. The licence has no effect until it has been so signed.

Gnath-shighniú an Cheadúnaí
Ordinary Signature of Licensee. .... R. Starkey

D.L. 2C.

George in a policeman's helmet.

Why would we have policeman's hats? Were we pretending to be policemen? I don't remember. But who's he going to fool? He's got his stage suit on. 'Oh yes, they'll never notice us now, we've got a policeman's hat on!'

I have an antique policeman's hat that George bought me, but it's not in this book.

HAT WELTRUF
FORMONT

John is wandering round in France.

It was very weird when we first went to Paris to play. We were used to screaming girls and Paris was full of boys. It was a very deep scream, which was really noticeable to us.

There's Brian in another hotel room.

Brian liked a laugh, but he was very posh compared to us. He had a furniture store with a record department in it, so he really knew records.

Brian did all the bookings, of course. He was the manager. All the tours, all the record sessions – everything we did, Brian was doing to move us on.

Paul's dad, Jim, with his pipe.

I love that picture. He came to a couple of gigs with us and he'd hang out in the hotel. He was a good lad. He was a piano player and taught Paul everything he knows.

Judy Martin – how beautiful.

What could she be doing? It looks like she's in the middle of prayers.

Sophie Hardy, the French actress, was doing a photo shoot, so I just hung out in the background and took shots as well. How beautiful.

Paul looks very French.

Paul and me.

It's on a timer, which is why we're looking strange. Timer shots are always weird because you don't know when it's going to go.

John looking thoughtful.

Every hotel ended up looking the same.

OF MUSIC AND

I love that shot, but it may not mean a lot to anyone but me.

Besides the fact that John has his glasses off, he is sitting in a typical 'him' pose. He had this weird way of sitting. The knee could go down to the floor and the leg right up to his shoulder! John and his fabulous loose hips. It's far out, isn't it? I can't do it. All you people reading this out there – can you do it? It's a competition.

George in the bathroom, getting ready.

He never took his shirt off while washing his hands and face – very Liverpool! I never had a bathroom in Liverpool. We used to just get washed in the sink. Just look at that bathroom – those were the days.

These are shots that no one else could have.

I just had the camera with me a lot of the time. That could be my empty plate next to John, with the knife and fork left on it.

That's a very nice portrait of John Lennon, looking rather spiffy.

Neil Aspinall, with John in the background.

Because it was dark in the room, they're just off-focus, but the moment is there and that's what's important.

This is a fun shot of Paul and Mal Evans.

When you're in hotels, you just look for things to do and have a bit of fun. By looking at the table, we've probably had a few drinks. That was in France. The clock and everything on the mantelpiece looks very français.

Paul was always playing the piano.

America was the dream of a lifetime.

George had been to the States the year before to visit his sister, and he'd gone to record stores, asking, 'Have you got the Beatles record?' And they were saying, 'Never heard of them.' So when he came back he said, 'Oh, it's going be so hard, they don't know us over there, you can't buy the records.' But by the time we got there to do *The Ed Sullivan Show*, we were Number One, thanks to Murray the K, Cousin Brucie and radio DJs like that. It was a frenzy and we never looked back. We thought, 'Wow, my God! We're here!'

The fluke of America was so great. We were getting off a plane from Sweden at Heathrow, and Ed Sullivan was getting off from New York. He just saw all the crowds on the roof and booked us, without even knowing what we did! And so we were booked to go to America, despite the fact we hadn't had a hit there. We played *The Ed Sullivan Show* again in Florida and it was great.

Ringo's *Ed Sullivan Show* Drum Kit, New York, February 9th 1964

Murray the K.

He broke The Beatles in America by playing our record on his *Submarine Race Watchers* show. He talked in a very weird language, which we couldn't understand, but it seemed like everyone in New York did. He came on that tour from New York to Washington and to Florida with us. We have to thank him; he was a great guy.

There's George, wearing one of Murray the K's T-shirts.

SUBMARINE
RACE WATCHERS

New York, February 1964

It says, 'Christine Keeler goes nudist plus Playgirls'!

So it makes no sense, really, but it's a great shot! I took it because Christine Keeler was 'well known' in Britain, but I didn't know she was 'well known' in America, too.

That's Phil Spector as a young man.

We loved Phil and he was an incredible producer. He made some great records and created the Wall of Sound, so he was one of our heroes. We met him when George and I lived on Green Street. There was a DJ who lived across the road that introduced us to him.

When we went to America, Phil came on the plane with us, but he was always nervous. He walked up and down the plane, all the way there and all the way back. It was really weird.

All the music we loved came from America. Liverpool was full of guys in the Merchant Navy, so all the American styles of clothing and their records would come to us first. Different music acts were known about in Liverpool before the rest of Britain.

OF NEW

Brian in the Beatle wig.

That's a great shot – look how he's laughing. I don't know if it's the negative, or if I shot it out of focus, or moved the camera. It didn't have to be clear; it captured the moment. I love that shot.

And then there's George Martin
in the Beatle wig.

And John, in God knows what.

What were we doing?

He was a great poser, Paul.

Mr Rock 'n' Roll, with the shades and the action.

All aboard!

Now this is the Seaboard Railroad Chair Car Attendant.

I think that's a great shot of Dežo.

The light is great because it's coming through the windows, but it's off his face. Do you see all the overcoats on the rack above him? Because it was so cold, we all had big overcoats on.

This is how we saw most of the world when it got big for The Beatles: out of a car window, going to or leaving somewhere.

That's just how it was. You had to get to the gig, and then get away from the gig to wherever you were going next. You'll find several of the shots in this book are from my point of view, looking out of a car window.

Being English, we thought that the cop with the gun was far out.

654
POLICE

YELLOW
CHEVROLET
YELLOW
CAB

'Wow, we're in America!'

I love this shot at the tollbooth.

ATTENDANT
WILL
MAKE CHANGE

They're looking at us, and I'm photographing them.

The first couple of years, we saw a lot of places from the car because we couldn't go out anywhere. We were just too big time. Everybody wanted a piece of us, so getting out was a big day.

Pensive George.

You should count the number of times we bought that heavy corduroy overcoat. We would always buy things in fours.

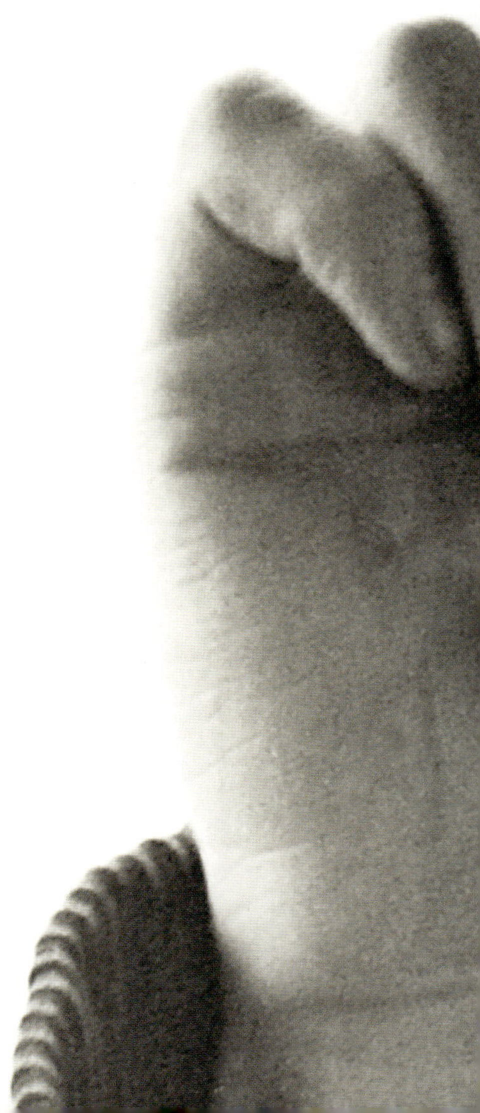

Miami, Florida, February 14th 1964

Whose legs are they?

I do not know, but I think it's a nice shot. We were on a boat in Florida. Somebody lent us their motor launch and we went out. They let me drive – I had the steering wheel – and I came in to port straight on! I didn't swing it sideways, and I broke the rail. But, if you were a Beatle, you could break the rails on anybody's boat in those days.

There's Bob Freeman and John, just hanging out in Florida.

We ended up hanging out with really nice guys. Bob was a very nice man and he took great shots, and that's exactly what we needed. He took some great album covers.

As you can see, Paul had a camera and George had a camera – we all had cameras.

There's George. If you look at the Beatles shots, in 90 percent of them, one of us is smoking. We were all smoking and drinking in those clean-cut Beatle days.

There's our hotel, the Deauville. We looked onto a big beach and you could see all the motor launches, bcats and yachts parked.

That's just one of Bob that I threw in.

As you can tell, I didn't take care of these slides. But they look arty to me.

California, August 1964

This is taken from the house we rented on our first trip to California.

This is a shot I took of John and Paul in the studio.

The first LP we made, *Please Please Me*, was all songs we did on the road. It took us 12 hours to record from start to finish – you know the story. John was so hoarse that we had to leave 'Twist and Shout' till the end, which made it so great. But recording for 12 hours wasn't a hardship. We were doing it; we were making a record. None of us was like, 'Oh, God,' we were like, 'Yeah!' It was exciting that we were going to have a piece of vinyl.

Every time they played us on the radio, they would tell us what time, because they'd have it all timed out, 'On the BBC, at 12.46pm, they're going to play it'. We'd be touring and we'd all be in the same car, so we'd stop, 'Let's pull over, yeah!' We used to celebrate every time one of our records was played or moved up the charts. In those days, it was just bigger than life.

I remember ending up in the studio for hours and hours and hours in the end. It was good, but I was the first person ever to put a back on a drum stool, so that I could just lean back a little. There was a lot of hanging-out time and I always wanted to be by the kit, ready if anyone got inspired. I had my little glass, a little drinkie and lots of cigarettes. I was like, 'I'm over here!'

Paul and John were in the box singing; I had the camera. I just got lucky and took these shots.

John and Paul would write the songs at the beginning, then George started, and then I joined in, too late I may add. We would usually play the track as a band, and then we'd overdub the tambourines or whatever instruments we used.

We made some incredible music. It's great how well it holds up – not the band, just the music itself. The songs are still relevant; the kids are listening to the music today. It worked. And there were many, many magic moments, when it really worked. I still get them now, onstage with the All-Starrs. When you're together, the band is together and the audience is together, it creates a magic moment that, unless you do it, you'll never understand. It's a magical, spiritual moment. You can feel it just lift your spirits. It's a good reason to go on tour.

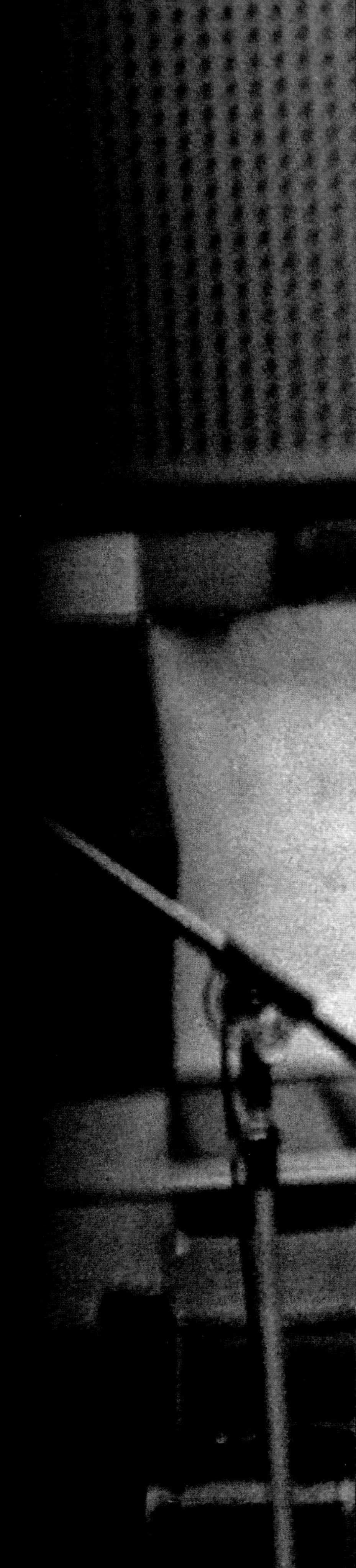

Another one of John and Paul.
They seem to have spotted me.

George liked to have a laugh.

There's Paul,
George Martin,
Mal and George.

Railway lines; just seemed a great shot at the time.

'Don't Pass Me By', first mentioned on *Top Gear*, July 1964

DONT PASS ME BY
DONT MAKE ME CRY
DONT MAKE ME BLUE
CAUSE YOU KNOW DARLIN I LOVE
ONLY YOU

YOU'L NEVER KNOW
IT HURT ME SO
O HOW I HATE TO SE YOU GO

YOU PASED ME BY
WHY MAKE ME ~~BLUE~~ CRY
" " " ~~CRY~~ BLUE

I SHOULD HAVE KNOWN BETER
THAN TO TRUST IN YOU
ALL MY FRENDS TOLD ME
YOU'D BE UNTRUE
BUT I DONT ~~KER~~ WHAT
THAY SAY
I NO YOUL CHANGE YOU WAY

Ringo

This is a shot of the cameraman on the set of *A Hard Day's Night*, showing what goes on around the making of a movie.

Filming *A Hard Day's Night* was very strange. We decided, 'Let's make a movie,' which was really far out. Before we started filming, we spent a lot of time with Alun Owen, the writer of the script. He came on tour with us, because that's what the film is all about, really.

I love the fact that my one big scene, the Ringo scene on the embankment, had about four pages of dialogue. But I wasn't very professional; I'd just come straight from a club! I couldn't remember my own name, never mind lines. First of all, I walked along with that kid and the continuity girl was shouting the lines at me. It all looked so fake, so in the end Dick Lester just said, 'Walk around and do what you do.' And that's how it worked. I was dejected because it was a day I didn't want to work, so I just moped around and made up the camera stuff. And it worked a treat! Dick was that free – that was what was so great. *A Hard Day's Night* was a great experience for me. From then on, I realised that I loved making movies.

In *Help!* I was the main character with the big ring. That film had the chase, the paint and the tiger, all these things! I thought, 'Oh yeah, this is good, I'm going to make a few movies.'

Candy was incredible. It was a really strange movie, all about this girl who just goes through life. *Candy* was just me, out on my own, without the boys. That was pretty strange, actually, but I wasn't there long. I don't know why they asked me, or how I got the part. I was just there, in Rome, with Richard Burton, Marlon Brando and Walter Matthau. To be around Marlon Brando was incredible. In those days, 1968, he was still hanging on doors and being Marlon Brando. I had to do lines with Richard Burton, who was so powerful that you could feel it off-camera. He was far out, but a miserable bugger. Sugar Ray Robinson (the boxer) was in it, and Elizabeth Taylor and I became great friends, too.

I did a movie called *Sextette* with Mae West in the Seventies. I played her Polish ex-husband. She was incredible to work with, but she had an earpiece in because she couldn't remember a single line! It revealed the mystery of movie-making to me. It was fun; we had a good time.

Mae took us out to dinner. When Mae went out to dinner, she would get there an hour early and have the staff change the lights so that she would look great in the restaurant! I had a party and I brought Mae as the guest of honour. She just sat there in her chair, and so many musicians were on their knees, wanting to talk to her.

It was good, but it faded out. I did some really bad TV stuff when I was not in control. Then, when I put the All-Starrs together in 1989, I realised that I didn't really want to be an actor. I wanted to be a musician.

There's Dick Lester, directing us in the train carriage on *A Hard Day's Night.*

He was really cool. I have great memories of Dick. He really understood that we were young boys and we had to take our medication! He knew when was enough filming for the day; Dick was a musician himself, so he understood the musician's life. The results we saw from Dick were great – just look at his camerawork and his focus.

Dick realised that we were four lads who had never made a film before, so he surrounded us with really great British actors. There was Wilfrid Brambell, of course, Norman Rossington and Victor Spinetti: a lot of guys that really knew what they were doing. And we were just like, 'Hey, let's go!'

The only problem with Wilfrid Brambell – though he was classically trained and a fine actor – was that he couldn't ad-lib, whereas we were used to ad-libbing. We didn't know any better, so the scene would end and we would carry on, but he would just be still.

Norman Rossington and John Junkin, who were in *A Hard Day's Night*.

The well-known comedian Eric Sykes.

He came to the set on *A Hard Day's Night* and let me take this portrait.

I like having the Beatle boot in there, with Dick being arty on the floor. The stance gives me the feeling that it's John being filmed.

Milan, June 1965

I think that's Milan, from the Paris to Milan tour.

George Harrison, c.1966

That's a great colour shot.

John, Cynthia, Maureen and I were on holiday in Tobago. I think that lady is getting the spines out of John's foot because he trod on a sea urchin – who knew they were dangerous?

Jumping for joy.

It's just a mark on the negative, but it looks like I'm doing all that with a cigarette in my mouth!

There's the little pieces and the money that we used to play Monopoly.

A shot of Japan from our hotel window.

To see something like that was just like, 'Oh my God! Look at this!' Of course behind it looks like any other city, but there's a bit of Japan right there.

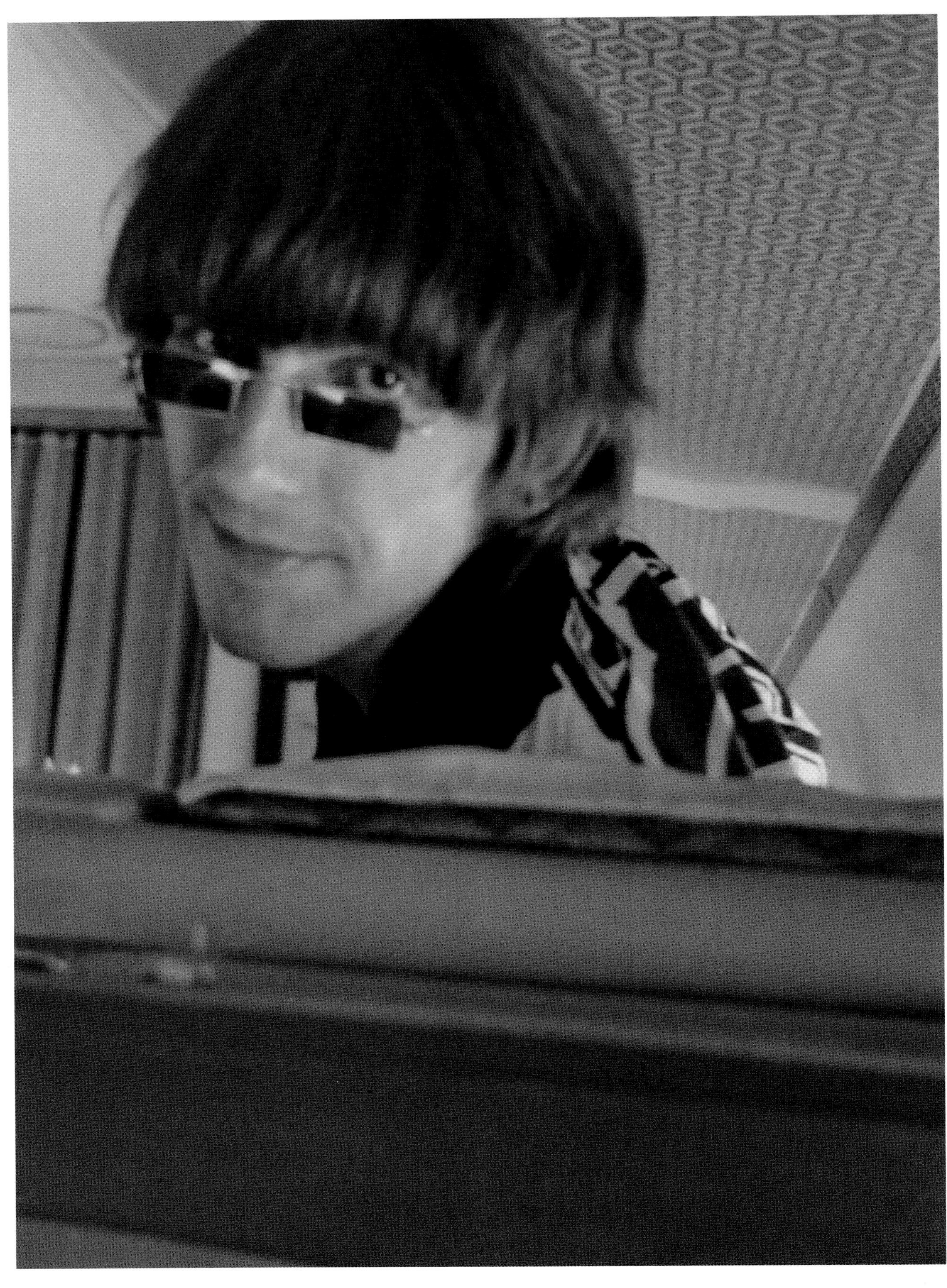

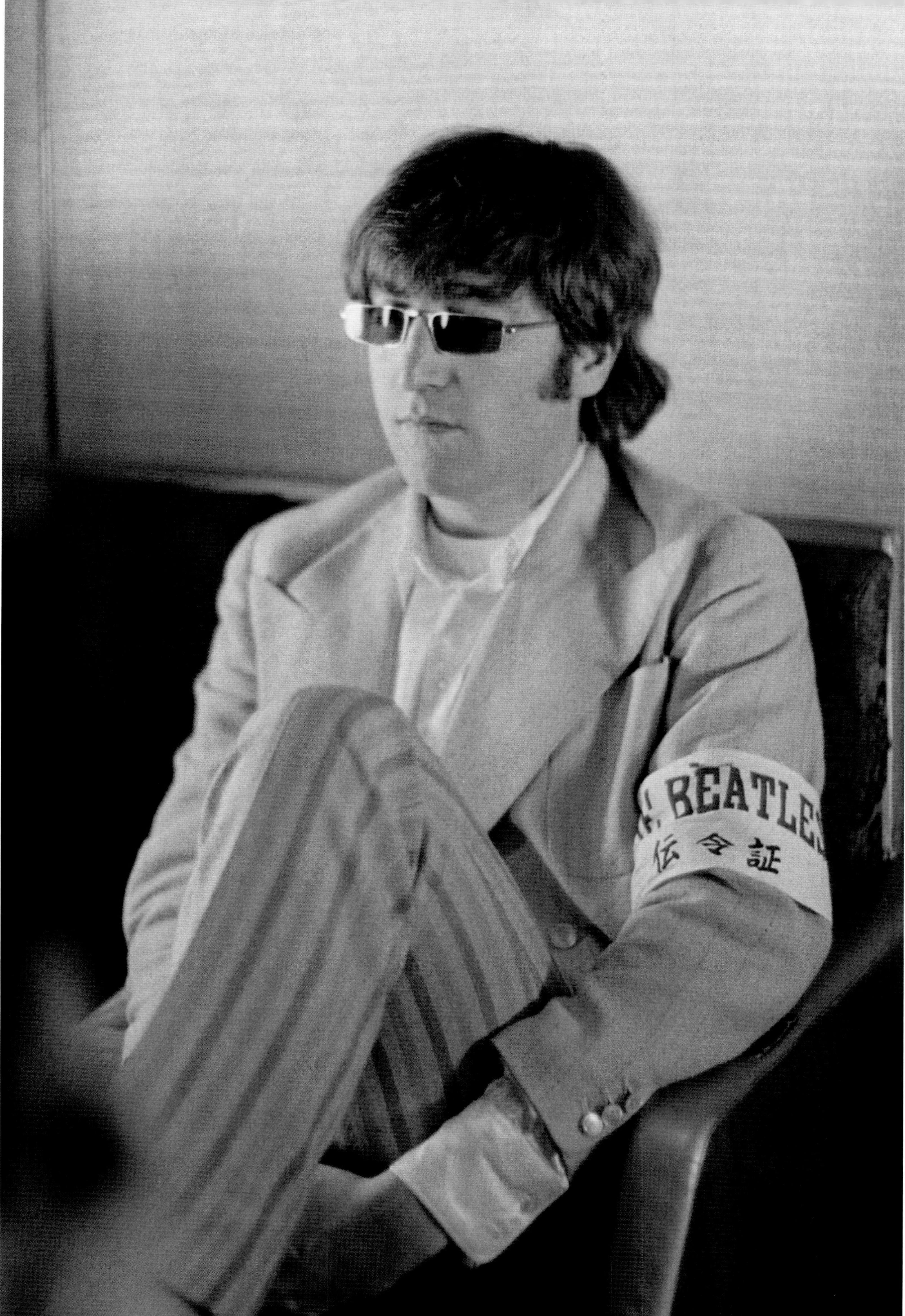
BEATLES
伝令証

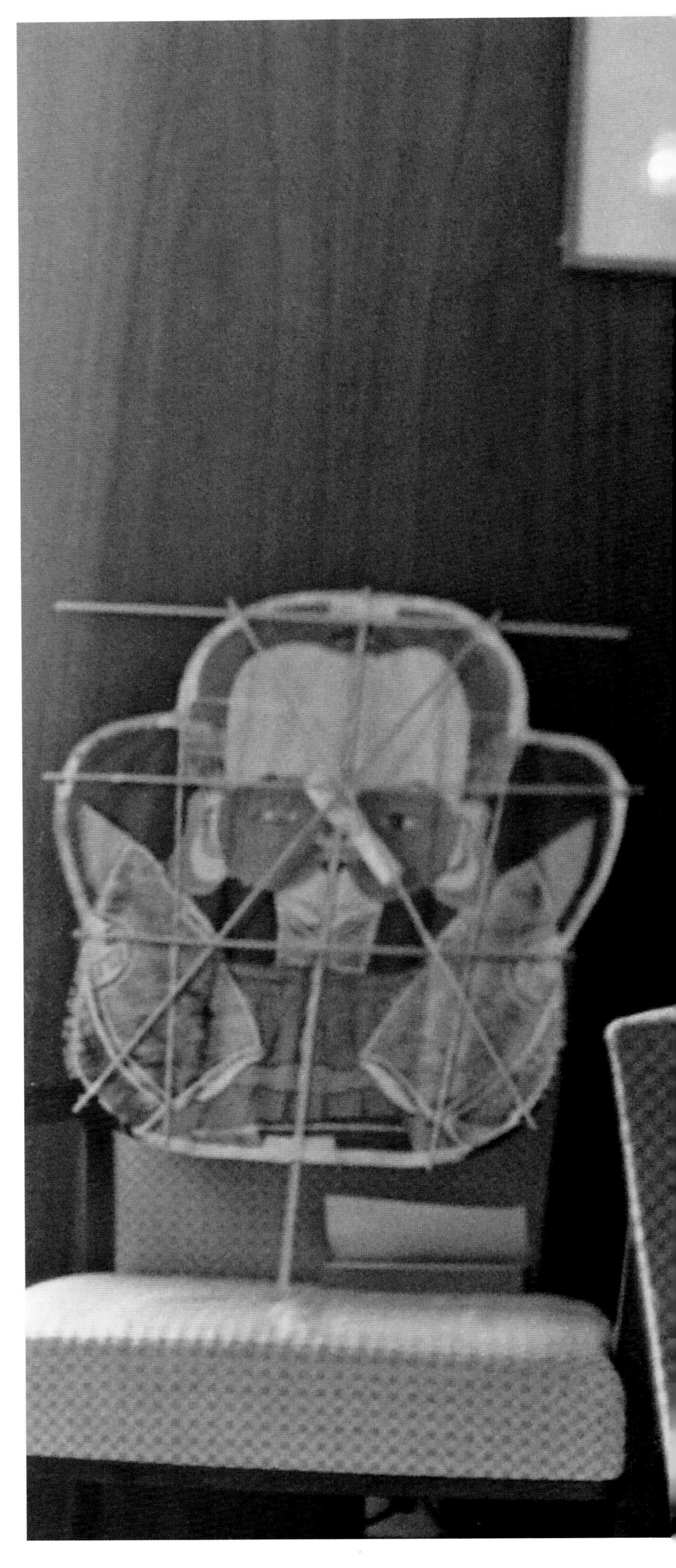

Greece, July 1967

ΜΟΥΣΑΜΑΔΕΣ

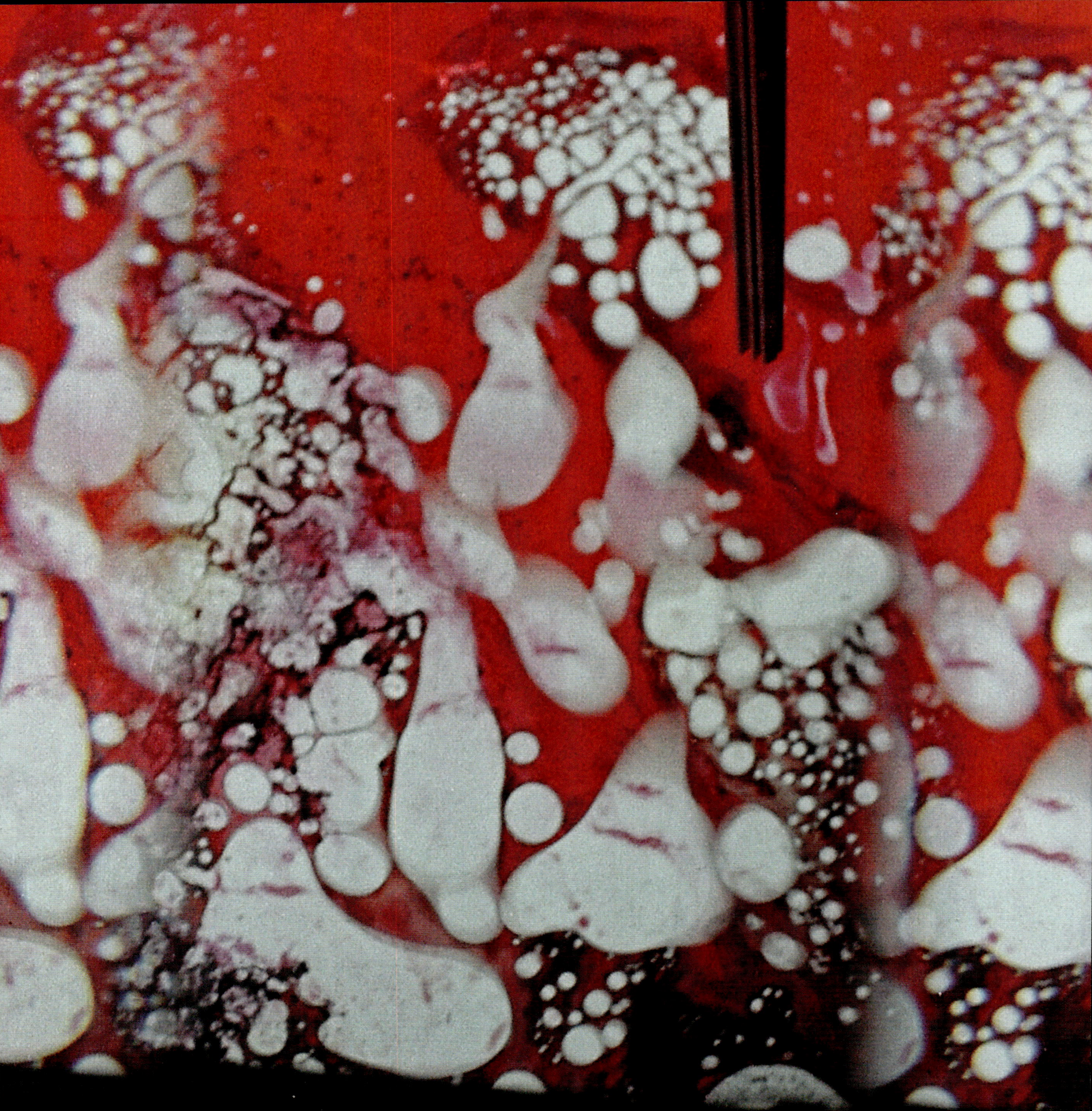

Substances came into play in the Sixties.

I used to make my own slides, with oil, water and coloured liquid. I would put them in a projector and the heat would start them moving, like it does in a lava lamp. Then I would project them, really big, onto the wall.

I also did quite a bit of projecting onto people. When we were filming the song 'Blue Jay Way' for *Magical Mystery Tour*, we ended up in my living room with me projecting images onto George. John was on my son's rocking horse, which just shows that you didn't have to get fancy to make a good video.

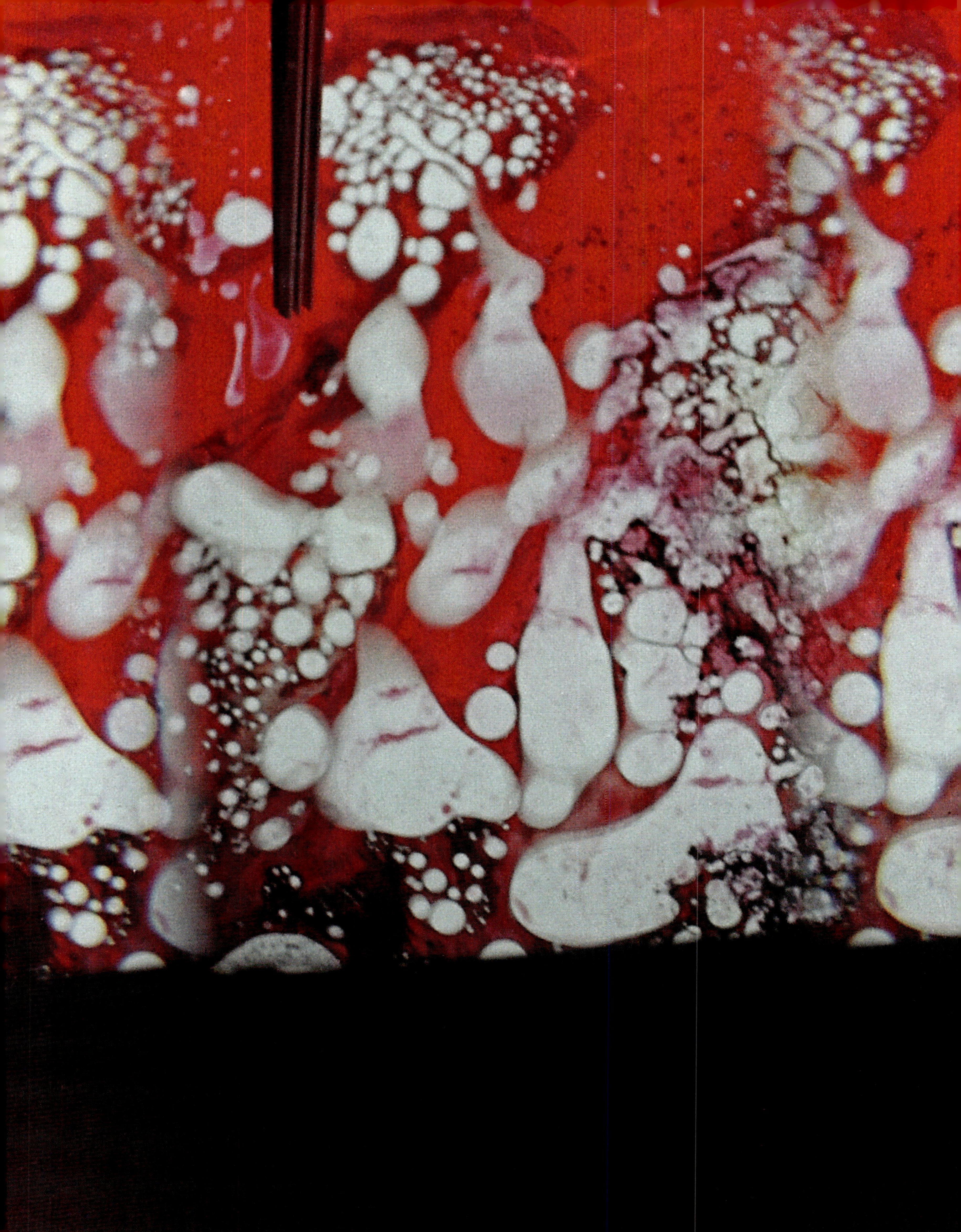

It looks like you're on your medication there, Mr Ringo!

Angry Cat!

That's a shot from a window of the house we had in Weybridge, looking down towards the grounds. When we had Zak in 1965, we decided that we couldn't live in London anymore. We wouldn't have been able to put him outside because people would have taken him as a memento! We moved to Weybridge and found this house, which we loved. It had about five acres. I've never been back; by now, it's probably been knocked down and replaced by four houses. But I've still got those lions outside my door.

A day out.

That's Julian Lennon and Zak Starkey on a boat trip, on a lake somewhere around Weybridge. We tried to live normal lives; we'd do things like take the kids to the playground. Both of them are musicians now.

That's Peter Sellers and me, back to back.

That was his house, and then I ended up with it. I didn't live there for very long, a year at most, and then I sold it to Stephen Stills. So it stayed in the musical family.

This is Ringo having breakfast.

That necklace has a story. My auntie bought it for me but, when we were in New York, kids jumped on our backs and stole it. I went on Cousin Brucie's radio show and said, 'I'll give you a kiss if you bring me back my necklace.' A girl turned up with the necklace, so I gave her a kiss, and I've still got it.

And there's another fish-eye; I love this one. My son Zak was about three here, and Jason had just been born.

The octopus is not in his garden, but it is an octopus.

I'd left the band because I couldn't stand it anymore. Peter Sellers lent me his yacht, and we went off and had a holiday in Sardinia. That's when I wrote 'Octopus's Garden'.

Jason was a baby and Stella, the nanny, was holding him as we walked through this pool. She said to me, 'Take the baby,' so I took the baby, and she had that thing wrapped around her leg! If it had been me, I would have tossed the baby and run, but she was so good. It's not going to kill you, but I wouldn't like to be somewhere and have something wrap itself around my leg! We took a photo of the octopus, and then I ended up writing a song about him.

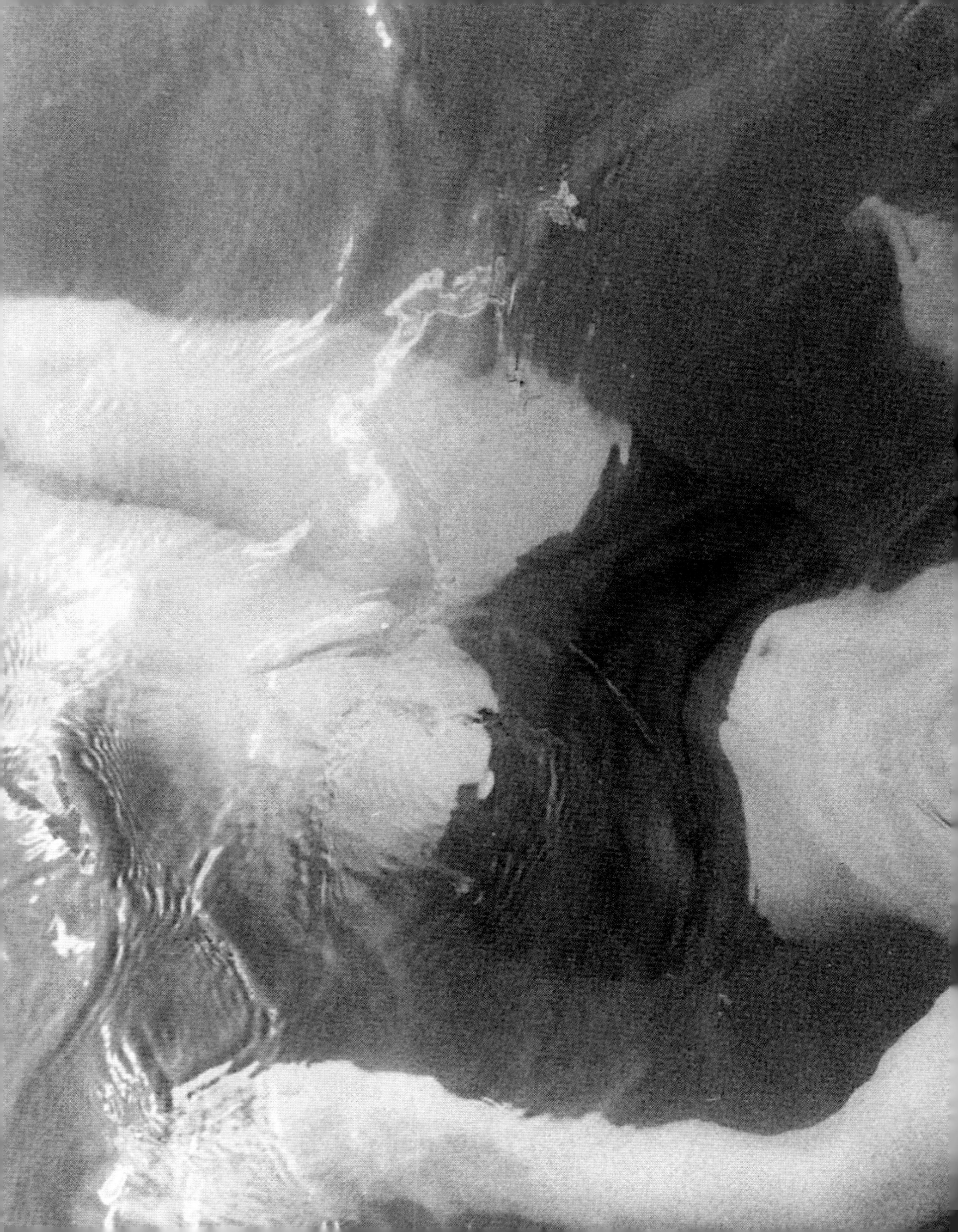

I wore that fake fur coat in *The Magic Christian*, the movie I did with Peter Sellers.

There was a guy working for us who gave me the book and said 'Peter owns the rights.' I just went to pieces and said, 'Come on, we've got to make this movie, it'll be great.' Terry Southern wrote it, which is how I got to know him. He was in the dressing room next to mine, on his own, typing away. They brought John Cleese and Graham Chapman in, too.

The maddest thing on that movie was that the guys who were financing it would come up to Joseph McGrath, the director, and say, 'We've got Yul Brynner.' And he'd say, 'What do you mean, you've got Yul Brynner?' 'We've got him, put him in the movie!' So they'd have to write Yul Brynner into the movie! They said, 'We've got Raquel Welch,' and suddenly there was a scene in the story where there's all these girls rowing on a ship and she's cracking the whip. She was a bombshell from LA. They would just meet all these actors and throw them in the movie. Then they'd bring the lines down for the actors on the day of filming.

It was a pretty strange way of working. I'd be sent to my room because Peter was having a tantrum, 'I think it's time you went back to your dressing room, Ringo.'

Blindman, June 1971

I did a movie called *Blindman*.

I was the brother of a Mexican gangster and I was a maniac. The joke is that I'd never ridden a horse before. It was a huge thing; the stirrup was eye-level! I would run to the horse and they'd cut, then they'd put me on the horse and I'd still look like a big tough guy.

Keith and I hung out a lot in the period of our lives when we were both on medication. The worst thing that happened was when we wrecked a railing in the Playboy Club. It was in the paper the next day, 'Keith Moon and Ringo Starr Destroy Playboy Club: £75 Worth of Damage'. We felt like wimps: only £75 worth of damage? Anyway, Vic Lownes, who ran the Playboy Club, let us go back.

Keith wasn't always mad, but he had mad moments, like everyone does. When we both lived in Ascot, I went over to Keith's house, and he'd bought a hovercraft and was just driving it around his garden.

We got a call one day, which was very harsh, 'You've got to come down – Keith is going mad and attacking things with a chisel.' He'd calmed down when Maureen and I got there, thank God. He was such a kind, loving guy, but he'd just go over the edge. The two sides of the moon.

All my children called him Uncle Keith. He'd come round dressed as Father Christmas, with the lady in his life as the Snow Queen. I had to stop him buying me gifts. He would send me a jukebox, but then a week later, I'd get the bill. I wanted to pick my own gifts!

We both loved rhinos, so I had two made and gave him one. A full-size fibreglass rhino. Keith put his rhino coming out of an arch, which you had to go through to get to his front door. One misty morning, the milkman came in his little electric buggy, and he turned and ran for his life! He thought that Keith was bound to have a real rhino.

I have my rhinoceros in my garden. We used to have parties with well-known pop stars of the day, which would go on till all hours. When dawn was breaking, I'd say, 'You've got to come and see the rhino.' I'd be walking through the grounds, calling, 'Come on, Ronnie. Here, Ronnie!' They would say, 'What? It's real?' and all hide behind my back! As if I'm actually going to have a real rhino. We had a lot of fun with that.

I'm still wearing all the rings, and this is the St Francis necklace that my auntie got me, which was ripped off in New York.

The fans didn't really attack us a lot, so these kids just got lucky. We would go out quite a bit, in those days, but it would start getting really crazy later on.

Harry Nilsson. Peace and love.

Harry was an incredible singer and songwriter, and I played on a couple of his records. I met him through the record *Aerial Ballet* and, from then on, we became really good friends. Actually, he was one of the few people that The Beatles allowed in to visit at Abbey Road.

There's lots of Barbara and me, of course.

Barbara and I met at LAX when I was checking in. We were flying to Mexico to do the *Caveman* movie. I was on one side of the check-in desk and she was on the other, being put on the plane by her boyfriend. I fell in love with her, and I couldn't do anything about it. I just fell in love, there anc then, and I'm still in love with her now. She tortured me for two months before I finally broke her down! Now we've been together for 33 years.

We're in Montserrat here.

There's George Martin; Steve Gadd, the drummer, and his lady; Paul and Linda; and Barbara and me. I think Paul was making a record and I played on it. A lot of times have all blended into one.

I did a couple of tracks in Montserrat myself, which Paul produced. They put Barbara and me in a very nice house, but we looked out of the window and there were giant iguanas – we were terrified. We ended up living in the studio, where they'd put the engineer to live. We threw him out and said, 'We're staying here; we're surrounded.' I didn't use a lot of the amenities! There was a waterfall somewhere that everyone went to see, but I missed that. It was a very narrow world we lived in, in those days.

These are two people kissing me: it looks like Paul and Linda.

I can even recognise them without their heads! Who took these shots? They are the worst shots ever; nobody's got a head!

My friendship with Paul goes way back. He was in that band we put together with John and George. I don't know why they were kissing me. Maybe they just couldn't help themselves. I'm dressed really smartly here, look at this: a tie with a pin.

There's Steve Gadd.

From the look of that big Elastoplast, it seems like something happened to my eye, but I don't remember what!

I think Barbara took this. It's so far out. In my head, that is me now: Mr Rock 'n' Roll with a guitar.

This is the Harmony guitar that I had when I went to Nashville. When Pete Drake was working on *All Things Must Pass*, George's record, I sent my car to pick him up from the airport. It had a lot of country cassettes in it, so he said, 'Hey, I see you like country music. You've got to come to Nashville and make a record.' I said, 'Nashville? I don't want to spend months in Nashville,' but he said, 'No, not months – we did *Nashville Skyline*, Bob Dylan's record, in two days.' So I went over and we made *Beaucoups of Blues*.

In the morning, we would listen to tracks and pick five. Then, in the afternoon, we'd record them. The next day we did the same, and it only took two days. That was the Nashville way: you just got up and did it.

I went to all those Nashville musicians with this guitar and said, 'I've got this song, "Coochy Coochy", in E – only E, no changes, just E!' And it turned out great. I was writing with one chord – how far out is that?

I play a bit of guitar and piano, but I've never put the time in to really learn them. They just give me some notes. Now, with synthesizers and computers, I can play in any key because you just press a button and play them all! By the way, 'Coochy Coochy' has just been covered by Ray Wylie Hubbard. I love Ray.

Tittenhurst Park, Ascot, 1983

Joe Walsh and Chris Stainton.

We were making *Old Wave* at Tittenhurst. Joe produced this record and Chris played on it. Chris is a great piano player.

We had a lot of happy moments recording at Tittenhurst. In the Eighties, Barbara and I got married and moved to England. There was already a studio in the house and I thought, 'Hey, that's a good idea. Bring Joe in and we'll do a record.' So that's what we did.

Old Wave was the first record of mine that Joe produced. I'd go into the library and start writing a song, then take it to Joe and we'd finish it together. We got on well. Working with Gary Brooker, John Entwistle and Ray Cooper was also great. They all came to the house and we hung out. We just got down to work and did our stuff, as best we could. I think this is the night that Joe said, 'We've worked very hard – we could have a mini-party.' Neither he nor I understood the term 'mini-party'.

That's me in LA with Keith Allison, in a car going somewhere.

Blue Suede Shoes: A Rockabilly Session with Carl Perkins, London, October 1985

This was for the Carl Perkins show that they put together in England.

Two of the records we made with The Beatles were Carl Perkins songs; George and I loved him.

This is Slim Jim and Lee Rocker from The Stray Cats – I don't know where their singer is; there's Dave Edmunds, who was in a couple of the All-Starr line-ups; and George and Eric.

Playing with Eric is always good. He's an incredible musician. That was my dream, to play drums with really great musicians, and it keeps unfolding. Eric played on 'While My Guitar Gently Weeps'. I thought it was incredible of George to give the lead to him. I saw Eric do that too, when I went to see him in LA. Carlos Santana got up to play with him, and he was blasting, so Eric gave him the shot. We're big enough to say, 'OK, you've got it, take this moment.' They're beautiful moments for me, musically.

With Joe Walsh, 1980s

Joe and me again, just hanging out.

The best All-Starr Band was in 1989.

It was special because it was the first line-up. I had sobered up and I was sitting around, wondering what to do with myself. I wasn't thinking of putting a band together. The first light went on when I remembered that I'm a musician. I'd become so derelict, for all those years, that I'd forgotten that. And then, out of the blue, a guy who I didn't know called me and said, 'Pepsi want to put you on tour.' I thought, 'Sure, but I'm going to take a lot of people with me.' I was so insecure because I'd never toured on my own before. I just opened my phone book and called these people, and they all said, 'Yes.' It was incredible!

EP THIS BOOK IN A SAFE PLACE
Its loss may cause you trouble
WALLET
RINGO
Photograph
Fotografia
Lichtbild
Photographie
Fotografera
Foto
Conmeditor
Valokuva
OPEN ONLY IN THE DARKROOM!
PHOTOGRAPHS
DO NOT BEND
CAN MAKE
PICTURES
ON
DAYS
OR EARLY OR LATE IN THE DAY
ANY SIZE ROLL OF
FILMS DEVELOPED
and
8
BORDER
PICTURES
LIKE THESE
ALL FOR ONLY
35¢
YOU
CAN GET
8
MORE
BORDER
PICTURES
LIKE THESE
FOR
ONLY
35¢
VERICHROME
FILMS
EXPOSURE—FILMS
1/3 More Film for Same Old Price
NAME
ORDER Nº
SIZE
SPOOLS
PRINTS
ENLGTS